asian soups

THE ESSENTIAL KITCHEN

asian soups

SUZIE SMITH

PERIPLUS

contents

asian soups

asian soups

Each well-respected world cuisine has in its repertoire a traditional soup ... blood-red beet (beetroot) borscht in Russia, the old bony potato gruels of Ireland, thick beany broths and bouillabaisse in France, clam-packed Manhattan chowders and Italian minestrone.

The typical soups of Asia span territories from Japan through Korea, Malaysia, Vietnam, China and Thailand, and while they are probably commonplace in local territory, to experience one from the "outside" is like seeing color for the first time. It is exciting to go headlong into the world of rich broths, noodles and herbs, and the tangy, spicy, delicious flavors that typify Asian soups.

Asian soups promote a well-being that is beyond the visual, the textural and the flavorful. For the most part, they are seen in Asian countries as health tonics or medicines vital for energy and restoring the body to its optimum state. In China, for example, chicken soup is thought to provide essential healing properties, and is given for recuperation to promote a stronger immune system.

Pho, the Vietnamese soup now famous all over the world, is also said to be a health-conscious choice, and is believed to be a "mind-clearing tonic." Pho means "your own bowl," and unlike other Asian meals where everything is shared, with this one, you are on your own—it is for you to design. Usually served for breakfast in order to fortify the mind and body for the day ahead, a classic pho consists of a rich anise-flavored beef or chicken broth made with caramelized onions and bones long simmered, poured over a mass of white rice noodles and meat with splashes of chili, hoisin or fish sauce and condiments that come in little dishes—bean sprouts, mint leaves, lemon and lime wedges and fresh chili peppers. Typically, the broth is poured over thin slices of raw lean beef—these cook as the broth comes to the table, for a minute or two, so that they are perfectly pink on the inside—or thin slices of steamed chicken. The beef and chicken components are adventurous; in Vietnam, fatty brisket and tripe are usual.

Laksa means "ten thousand," referring to the enormous variety of vegetables that can be added to the soup as condiments. (You could add almost anything from pineapple and deep-fried tofu to eggs!) Laksa is from the cuisine called Nonya. This is an invention of the Chinese people living in Malaysia—they brought to Malaysia their traditional Chinese cuisine, which slowly but surely became influenced by the hotter, spicier cuisine of Malaysia. In Malaysia, laksa is sold only at markets or at hawkers' stands, and is traditionally a snack eaten by "ladies" in the afternoon. Typically, it consists of rice noodles in a sour-flavored fish soup made from a paste that is a curious blend of dried shrimp, nuts and spices, including turmeric, which gives it its glorious sunshine color. While a seafood laksa is the most authentic style, chicken and vegetables, though perhaps "Westernized" through Asian eyes, are also fabulous.

As with the pho, the condiments are added at the end or sprinkled on top, the crowning glory being the beautiful crisp onions—you can find them in Chinatown, but they are twice as satisfying to make at home out of slivers of shallots (French shallots).

Hot and sour flavors and coconut milk bases typify Thai soups. Kaffir lime leaves and lime juice are imperative for giving that distinctive sour tang to the soups. If you cannot find fresh kaffir lime leaves, grow a tree or buy dried ones

(they will suffice if you double the quantity you would use of fresh ones). Kaffir limes, which are often difficult to find, are a strange knobbly-surfaced fruit. If you do chance upon them, use the zest as you would lime zest in the recipes. Another delicious flavor in Thai cooking comes from galangal, a root that is not dissimilar to ginger but is slightly tangier (another citrusy addition). Substitute galangal for ginger or vice versa, depending on which you come across. The spice and citrus of Thai soups stimulate the appetite during hot seasons and cool the body—if you eat something hot, afterward you will feel cooler. Relative to other Asian soups, though, Thai soups are lighter and do not have noodles.

In Japan, soups are based on clear stocks or are made with fermented beans and rice or barley (miso). Typical of Japanese cuisine, they are very simple in appearance and flavor and are virtually fat free. However, like pho and laksa, many have noodles and a meat topping, commonly beef or pork. Japanese soups seem bland by contrast with Chinese, Vietnamese and Malaysian soups because spices are not used to the same extent.

Korean cuisine falls between the cuisines of China and Japan—it is more complex than Japan's but not as sophisticated and rich as China's. Unlike people of both those countries, however, Koreans are very very fond of chili peppers. In all the recipes following, feel free to add as much or as little chili as you desire; in terms of flavor, chili peppers do not make a big difference, but they are a wonderful heat-giving ingredient.

Asian soups are a big adventure. Like all soups, they are humble, fundamental and deeply satisfying, and they require no great culinary skills. Shopping is important—most of the ingredients can be purchased in the supermarket, but the more unusual or unfamiliar ones, such as galangal and kaffir lime leaves, may require a trip to an Asian market or local Chinatown.

Even more important is the quality of the stock you use. Undoubtedly, making your own will give you a stock that is superior to any store-bought product, as most purchased varieties have some kind of coloring and/or preservatives, and definitely do not have the Asian flavors that you can add to your own. If you do use store-bought stock, simmering it with ginger and garlic or lemongrass and kaffir lime leaves adds more flavor. The result is infinitely more satisfying and would no doubt be a much better equivalent to the "real thing". Remember, the right ingredients are especially good for the body and soul. And what you put in is what you get out!

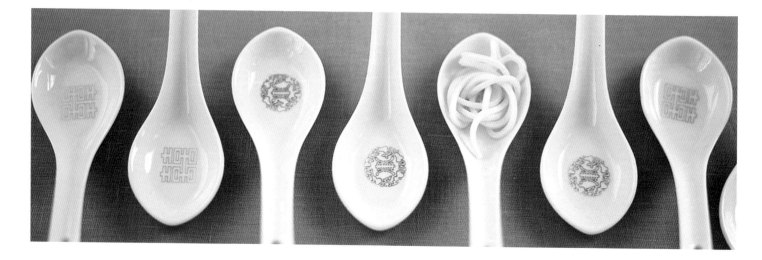

asian soups

In Asia, eating soup is a communal activity. Whether in a market stall or at home, one is bound to be surrounded by people with big bowls, clicking chopsticks and little spoons (for slurping the liquid).

For many Asian meals, "don't use your fingers" is not an admonishment; in fact, eating with your fingers and feeling the textures are integral to the experience. For obvious reasons, however, soups are eaten strictly with spoons and chopsticks, something that must be seen to be believed if you really want to know how to do it properly. It is a continuum of motion between the chopsticks and the spoon—the chopsticks picking up the noodles, meat, fish or vegetables and the spoon quickly following with the liquid. Of course, there is nothing to stop you using a spoon and a fork.

Whichever the country of origin, whichever the soup, a big china bowl is absolutely essential. The reason dinnerware is often referred to as "china" is because the material for plates and bowls was first made in China. They were created from porcelain, a hard-body ceramic consisting of a white clay that was typical to China. Chinatown is a good place to start looking if you want a pile of reasonably priced, durable bowls (porcelain is quite strong and chip resistant)—you will also find those little fat china spoons and chopsticks there. Though not made of the finest china, they are another invaluable addition to your tableware supply. Most Asian markets also carry the finer-glazed Japanese porcelains and the typical blue-patterned bowls in squatter shapes from Thailand. Some of the soup bowls have lids, which adds an authentic touch and keeps the soup warm.

You can make a lot of the soups a colorful styling affair by putting the garnishes and condiments in separate little bowls and setting them on the table so diners can construct their own soup. This is especially the case for phos and laksas, where the condiments are colorful and served in a separate bowl and need to be added as the soup is consumed.

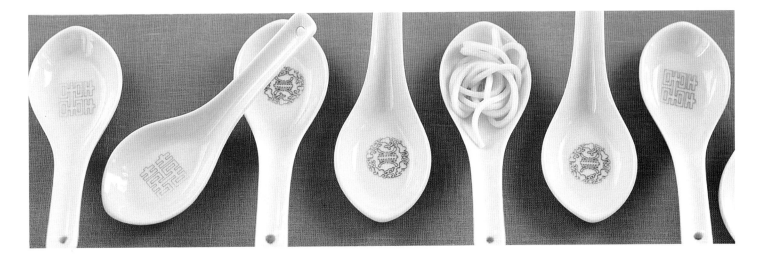

ingredients

GINGER AND GARLIC

Ginger and garlic

Most recipes in this book call for ginger and garlic. Use only fresh ingredients and chop or grate them yourself. Powdered forms of both are no substitute. Be especially careful not to substitute ground ginger, which has a significantly different flavor. Many stores sell chopped garlic and ginger in jars. While the flavor is better than dried and they will suffice, nothing will ever surpass the real, fresh thing.

Lemongrass

This tall, lemon-scented grass that grows in clumps and resembles a miniature leek is used in many Asian recipes. Lemongrass is an invaluable ingredient, especially in Thai soups and laksa paste, as it intensifies the sour citrus flavor. Use only the bottom 3 inches (7.5 cm) of each stalk. The rough outer leaves are usually discarded, and the more tender center is used finely chopped or in long strips that are removed from the soup before serving but which have infused it with their flavor. Dried lemongrass and lemongrass powder are available, but most of the flavor has been lost in the processing and packaging.

LEMONGRASS

Limes and lemons

Both are essential ingredients in Asian cooking, especially for providing the "sour" flavor prevalent in many soups. Lemons and limes are used as a seasoning in Asia much as Westerners use salt and pepper. Substituting store-bought, pre-packaged lemon and lime juice will give a poor result.

Shallots (French shallots)

Small, round, pinkish purple shallots, with golden exteriors, add a sweet oniony flavor to dishes—fresh or deep-fried—as they also do when used as a garnish for laksas. Packets of already fried crisp shallots or onions are generally available in Chinatown or in Asian markets.

SHALLOTS (FRENCH SHALLOTS)

Miso

Miso is a thick paste made from fermented and processed soybeans. The paste is the base for miso soup, which is made by pouring boiling water over the miso and stirring until it is dissolved. Miso has a salty flavor and is rich in vitamin B.

Deep-fried tofu

Otherwise known as bean curd, tofu is made from soybean milk and is extremely rich in protein. Originally used by the Chinese, tofu is now widely used throughout Asia. Deep-fried tofu—firm tofu that has been deep-fried—is usually used in soups as it holds its shape and does not fall apart.

Star anise

An important ingredient in pho stocks, star anise is a dark brown star-shaped spice with a flavor like aniseed.

MISO

DEEP-FRIED TOFU

STAR ANISE

TURMERIC

Turmeric

For laksa paste, turmeric is used in its dried form, which is a rich yellow powder. Fresh turmeric looks similar to ginger (it is a member of the same family), but has a yellow flesh. The flavor of turmeric is very subtle, but for making color, a little bit goes a long way.

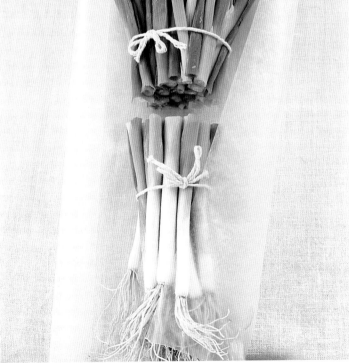

SCALLIONS

Scallions

Used as a herb to flavor dishes, especially as a garnish. These are sometimes known as green onions, spring onions, or, rather confusingly, as shallots (in Australia).

Fish sauce

Fish sauce, like soy sauce, is used in Asian countries in the same way that Westerners use salt. It is a very important ingredient for flavoring many Asian dishes, particularly Thai. It is a clear, amber-colored liquid that is drained from salted, fermented fish.

Chicken stock

1 chicken, whole, about 2 lb (1 kg)

1 large onion, roughly sliced

1 large carrot, peeled and chopped

2 celery stalks, chopped

5 cilantro (coriander) stems, including roots

1 teaspoon sea salt

8 black peppercorns

10 cups (80 fl oz/2.5 L) water

Place chicken, onion, carrot, celery, cilantro, salt and peppercorns in a large saucepan and cover with water. Place over medium–high heat and bring liquid to a boil.

Reduce heat to medium–low and simmer for 1–1½ hours, skimming surface occasionally to remove scum and fat.

Remove saucepan from heat. Remove chicken and strain liquid. Allow stock to cool completely, then remove remaining fat from surface.

Makes 8 cups (64 fl oz/2 L)

Hints

To enhance the Asian flavor of this stock, add 5 or 6 slices fresh ginger or galangal, or a 2-inch (5-cm) piece of lime zest (rind), or 2 fresh (or 4 dried) kaffir lime leaves. Stock can be refrigerated for 5 days, or frozen for up to 3 months. Chicken meat may be pulled from bones and reserved for another use.

Fish stock

about 2 lb (1 kg) heads and bones of 2 medium-
    sized white-fleshed fish

2 tablespoons light olive oil

1 large onion, roughly chopped

1 large carrot, peeled and roughly chopped

2 celery stalks, with leaves, roughly chopped

3 stems flat-leaf parsley

3 stems cilantro (coriander), preferably including
    roots

3 fresh or 6 dried kaffir lime leaves, optional

8 black peppercorns

1 teaspoon sea salt

Wash fish heads and bones well, removing any gills. Chop bones so that they fit into a large pot.

Heat oil in a large pot over high heat for 1 minute. Add fish heads and bones and cook, stirring and turning heads and bones, until any remaining flesh starts to cook and is slightly golden, 4–5 minutes.

Add remaining ingredients and stir to combine. Add enough water to cover bones completely (approximately 8 cups/64 fl oz/2 L) and bring liquid to a steady simmer. Reduce heat to medium and simmer for 25 minutes. Skim any scum from surface as stock simmers.

Strain liquid through a very fine sieve. If you don't have a very fine sieve, line your sieve with a double layer of damp cheesecloth (muslin). Discard solids.

Allow stock to cool then cover with plastic wrap and refrigerate if not using immediately.

Makes 8 cups (64 fl oz/2 L)

Hints

Stock can be refrigerated for 2 days. If stored in tightly covered containers, it can be frozen for 2 months.

Laksa paste

³/₄ cup (4 oz/125 g) dried shrimp (prawns)

12 dried red chili peppers

6–8 scallions (shallots/spring onions) about
  6¹/₂ oz (200 g), roughly chopped

6 cloves garlic

4-inch (10-cm) piece fresh ginger, peeled and
  roughly chopped

2 teaspoons dried shrimp paste

2 stalks lemongrass, bottom 3 inches (7.5 cm)
  only, chopped

¹/₂ cup (3 oz/90 g) candlenuts or blanched
  almonds

1 tablespoon ground turmeric

¹/₂ cup (4 fl oz/125 ml) light olive oil

Place shrimp and chili peppers in a bowl and add enough boiling water to cover. Allow to stand for 15 minutes. Drain, then place shrimp and chili pepper mixture in a food processor with remaining ingredients. Process mixture to a fine paste, 2–3 minutes. Transfer paste to a bowl or sterilized jar, then cover and refrigerate.

Makes 1½ cups (12 oz/375 g) (enough for 3 laksa recipes, each serving 4)

Hint

Paste can be refrigerated for up to 10 days.

Pho beef stock

10 lb (5 kg) beef bones

1 teaspoon sea salt

2-inch (5-cm) piece fresh ginger

3 medium yellow (brown) onions

2 star anise seeds

6 cloves

1 teaspoon black peppercorns

1 cinnamon stick

5 cardamom pods

2 tablespoons fish sauce

Place beef bones in a large stockpot. Cover with cold water, place over high heat and bring to a boil. Boil for 2 minutes. Strain liquid through a large sieve or colander. Discard liquid and keep bones. Return bones to stockpot. Cover with cold water, add salt and bring to a boil over high heat. Reduce heat to medium–low and simmer for 3–4 hours.

While waiting for the water to boil, grill ginger and onions over a gas flame or under a very hot broiler (grill). For ginger, hold with tongs, turn until skin can be easily peeled away, about 3 minutes. For onions, hold each with tongs and turn over flame until skin and outer layer are burnt and slightly soft, 3–4 minutes. Remove and discard burnt outer layer.

Heat a frying pan over high heat and lightly roast anise seeds by swirling them in pan for 2 minutes.

Add ginger, onions, anise seeds and remaining ingredients to simmering stock.

After stock has simmered 3–4 hours, strain. Discard solids and skim off any residue.

Use stock immediately for making a pho, or keep, refrigerated and covered, for up to 4 days, or frozen (in covered containers) for 1 month.

Makes 8 cups (64 fl oz/2 L)

Hints

For making a chicken stock for a pho, substitute 1 large, whole chicken and 2 lb (1 kg) of chicken bones for the beef bones. Instead of simmering 3–4 hours, simmer for 1½ hours.

Chicken and green vegetable pho

1 whole chicken, about 3 lb (1.5 kg)

3 medium onions

3 cloves garlic

2-inch (5-cm) piece fresh ginger

2 star anise seeds

12 oz (375 g) fresh egg noodles

8 oz (250 g) snow peas (mange-tout)

8 oz (250 g) small green beans

$^1/_4$ cup ($^1/_4$ oz/7 g) cilantro (coriander) leaves

chili paste, for serving

Place chicken in a large pot with 10 cups (80 fl oz/2.5 L) water. Place over high heat and bring to a boil. Immediately reduce heat to medium–low and simmer chicken for 1½ hours.

As soon as chicken is simmering, grill onions, garlic and ginger (all in their skins) over a gas flame or under a very hot broiler (grill), turning to brown all sides. The skins will char. Peel away and discard charred skin and add onions, garlic and ginger to chicken. Add anise seeds.

After chicken has simmered for 1½ hours, carefully remove from liquid and set aside. Strain liquid and discard solids. Place liquid in a large saucepan over medium–low heat and keep warm until ready to serve.

Cut chicken into serving pieces and set aside.

Bring a large saucepan of water to a boil. Add noodles and cook until tender, 5–7 minutes. Drain noodles, then rinse them under very hot water and set aside.

Bring a saucepan half filled with water to a boil. Add snow peas and green beans and cook until tender, 2–3 minutes. Drain and set aside.

Place noodles in individual bowls. Ladle hot stock over noodles. Accompany with small bowls of chicken, peas, beans, cilantro and chili paste. Each diner assembles his or her own bowl.

Serves 4

CHICKEN AND GREEN VEGETABLE PHO

Chicken and sweet corn soup

2 teaspoons light olive or vegetable oil

1 large yellow (brown) onion, sliced

1 lb (500 g) skinless, boneless chicken thigh meat,
   cut into 1-inch (2.5-cm) cubes

4 oz (125 g) sliced ham, cut into thick strips

2 cloves garlic, chopped

2-inch (5-cm) piece fresh ginger, peeled and
   grated

4 cups (1½ lb/750 g) fresh or frozen corn kernels

8 cups (64 fl oz/2 L) chicken stock (see page 14
   for step-by-step instructions)

½ teaspoon white pepper, or to taste

sea salt to taste

1 small red (Spanish) onion, cut into petals,* for
   garnish

4 small red chili peppers, cut to form flowers,**
   for garnish

8 baby sweet corn cobs, fresh or canned,
   for garnish

Heat oil in a large saucepan over medium–high heat. Add onion and cook until soft and slightly golden, about 5 minutes, stirring occasionally. Add chicken cubes, ham strips, garlic and ginger and continue to cook for 2–3 minutes. Add corn kernels and cook for 2 minutes. Add stock and bring mixture to a boil. Reduce heat to medium and simmer until corn is soft, about 10 minutes. Season to taste with white pepper and salt.

Ladle into individual bowls and garnish with red onion petals, chili pepper flowers and baby corn cobs.

* Halve onion, cutting from root end to top, then cut each half, from just above root end to top, into thick wedges. The root end should hold wedges together. Separate layers, without breaking from root end, so you have individual petals.
** Cut chili peppers in strips, from tip to just next to stem, and place in a bowl of ice water in refrigerator until strips curl, 20–30 minutes.

Serves 4

CHICKEN AND SWEET CORN SOUP

Chicken coconut soup

1 tablespoon light olive oil

2-inch (5-cm) piece fresh ginger, peeled and grated

3 cloves garlic, crushed

2 small red chili peppers, or to taste, finely chopped

4 cilantro (coriander) roots, finely chopped

5 scallions (shallots/spring onions), green and white parts, trimmed and finely chopped

5 oz (150 g) button mushrooms, trimmed and halved if large

2-inch (5-cm) piece galangal, sliced

1 stalk lemongrass, bottom 3 inches (7.5 cm) only, cut into 2-inch (5-cm) lengths

3 tablespoons lime juice

1 tablespoon fish sauce

4 cups (32 fl oz/1 L) chicken stock (see page 14 for step-by-step instructions)

2 cups (16 fl oz/500 ml) coconut milk

4 fresh or 8 dried kaffir lime leaves

2 skinless, boneless chicken breasts, 6 oz (180 g) each, thinly sliced

1/2 cup (1/2 oz/15 g) cilantro (coriander) leaves, for garnish

Heat oil in a large saucepan over medium heat. Add ginger, garlic, chili peppers, cilantro roots and scallions and cook over medium heat, stirring occasionally, for 5 minutes. Add mushrooms, galangal and lemongrass and cook for 3 minutes. Add lime juice, fish sauce, chicken stock, coconut milk and kaffir lime leaves. Increase heat to high and bring mixture to a steady simmer. Reduce heat to medium and simmer for 15 minutes. Add chicken slices and cook until chicken is cooked through, about 5 minutes. Adjust seasonings—add more fish sauce if soup is not salty enough, or more lime juice if it is not tangy enough.

Remove lime leaves, galangal and lemongrass before serving. Ladle soup into individual bowls and serve sprinkled with cilantro leaves.

Serves 4

CHICKEN COCONUT SOUP

Chicken laksa

2 large skinless, boneless chicken breast halves,
 1 lb (500 g) total

2 tablespoons light olive oil

sea salt and freshly ground black pepper

$1/2$ cup (4 oz/125 g) laksa paste (see page 18 for
 recipe)

3 tablespoons lemon or lime juice

3 cups (24 fl oz/750 ml) coconut milk

3 cups (24 fl oz/750 ml) chicken stock (see page 14
 for step-by-step instructions)

2 cups (10 oz/300 g) cherry tomatoes

6 oz (180 g) thick dried rice noodles

1 cup (5 oz/150 g) pineapple pieces, about $1/2$ inch
 (12 mm)

1 small cucumber, peeled and sliced

2 tablespoons chopped fresh mint leaves

$1/4$ cup cilantro (coriander) leaves

$1/4$ cup (2 oz/60 g) crisp fried shallots (French
 shallots) (see page 58 for recipe)

Brush chicken breasts with 2 teaspoons oil. Heat a cast-iron frying pan or stove-top grill pan over high heat until very hot, about 5 minutes. Cook chicken breasts until tender and cooked through, 4–5 minutes on each side. Season with salt and black pepper. Remove and set aside.

Heat remaining oil in a large saucepan over medium–high heat. Stir in laksa paste and cook until fragrant, 4–5 minutes, stirring frequently. Add lime juice, coconut milk and chicken stock and stir until mixture is thoroughly combined. Reduce heat to medium and simmer for 10 minutes. Add tomatoes and simmer for 5 minutes.

Place noodles in a large bowl and add boiling water to cover. Allow to stand until noodles are soft, about 3 minutes. Drain noodles, rinse under warm water and set aside.

Slice chicken breasts into thin slices. Spoon noodles into individual bowls and ladle soup over them. Top with chicken slices and remaining ingredients, finishing with a sprinkling of shallots. Serve immediately.

Serves 4

CHICKEN LAKSA

Chicken noodle soup

2 teaspoons light olive oil

1 medium white onion, very thinly sliced

1 tablespoon soy sauce, or to taste

8 cups (64 fl oz/2 L) chicken stock (see page 14 for step-by-step instructions)

1-inch (2.5-cm) piece fresh ginger, peeled and sliced

2 medium carrots, peeled and sliced into rounds or flowers*

white pepper to taste

8 oz (250 g) thin egg noodles

1½ cups (8 oz/250 g) shredded, cooked chicken breast meat

3½ oz (105 g) sliced ham, cut into thin strips

2 tablespoons finely chopped cilantro (coriander), for garnish

Heat oil in a large saucepan over medium–high heat. Add onion and cook, stirring frequently, until onions begin to soften, 3–4 minutes. Add soy sauce, chicken stock and ginger, increase heat to high and bring mixture to a boil. Add carrot flowers, reduce heat to medium and simmer until carrots are just soft, about 10 minutes. Season to taste with white pepper and extra soy sauce if desired.

Meanwhile, bring a large saucepan half filled with water to a boil and add noodles. Cook until noodles are tender, 5–7 minutes (time depends on noodle thickness). Drain noodles and set aside.

Add chicken and ham to soup and cook until heated through, about 2 minutes.

Place cooked noodles in individual bowls and ladle soup over top. Serve immediately, sprinkled with chopped cilantro.

* Cut carrots into slices ⅛ inch (3 mm) thick. Make flowers using small, flower-shaped cookie (pastry) cutter.

Serves 4

CHICKEN NOODLE SOUP

Quick-and-easy chicken laksa

1½ tablespoons peanut oil

7 oz (220 g) skinless, boneless chicken thigh meat,
  sliced into strips

2 teaspoons chili paste or sambal oelek

3 cloves garlic, minced, or 2 teaspoons prepared
  crushed garlic

2-inch (5-cm) piece fresh ginger, peeled and
  finely grated, or 2 teaspoons prepared crushed
  ginger

1 teaspoon ground coriander

½ teaspoon turmeric

1 teaspoon dark brown sugar

grated zest (rind) of 1 lemon (about 2 teaspoons)

¼ cup (2 fl oz/60 ml) lemon juice

1 tablespoon fish sauce

6 cups (48 fl oz/1.5 L) chicken stock (see page 14
  for step-by-step instructions)

2 cups (16 fl oz/500 ml) coconut milk

8 oz (250 g) fresh egg noodles

8 oz (250 g) deep-fried tofu

5 oz (150 g) bean sprouts, trimmed

1 small cucumber, sliced and quartered

3 scallions (shallots/spring onions), sliced

½ cup (½ oz/15 g) cilantro (coriander) sprigs

lime wedges, optional, for serving

Heat oil in a large saucepan over medium–high heat. Add chicken strips and cook, turning frequently, until slightly brown, about 4 minutes. Add chili paste, garlic, ginger, coriander, turmeric, brown sugar and lemon zest and cook, stirring, until spices are aromatic, 3–4 minutes. Add lemon juice, fish sauce, chicken stock and coconut milk. Increase heat to high and bring mixture to a steady simmer. Reduce heat to medium–low and simmer for 15 minutes.

Meanwhile, bring a large saucepan of water to a boil and add noodles. Cook until noodles are tender, 5–7 minutes, then drain and rinse noodles under very hot water.

Place noodles in individual bowls and ladle soup over top. Top with tofu, bean sprouts, cucumber, scallions and cilantro and serve immediately. Serve with lime wedges if desired.

Serves 4

QUICK·AND·EASY CHICKEN LAKSA

Hot and sour chicken soup

FOR TOM YUM STOCK

2 tablespoons vegetable oil

1 teaspoon chili powder

2 tablespoons dried shrimp (prawns)

1 stalk lemongrass, bottom 3 inches (7.5 cm) only, chopped

1 clove garlic, chopped

4 black peppercorns

1 teaspoon galangal powder or 1 tablespoon chopped fresh galangal

1 red chili pepper

1 green chili pepper

3 fresh or 6 dried kaffir lime leaves

2 tablespoons fish sauce

2 tablespoons lime juice

$1/2$ teaspoon shrimp paste

2 teaspoons finely grated lime zest (rind)

8 cups (64 fl oz/2 L) chicken stock (see page 14 for step-by-step instructions)

FOR SOUP

2 teaspoons peanut oil

1 red (Spanish) onion, sliced

1 medium carrot, julienned

skinless, boneless chicken breasts, 8 oz (250 g) each, sliced

3 oz (90 g) small button mushrooms, sliced (optional)

4 fresh or 8 dried kaffir lime leaves

lime juice and fish sauce to taste

4 basil sprigs, for garnish

To make tom yum stock: Heat vegetable oil in a large saucepan over medium heat until hot, about 1 minute. Add chili powder and stir until oil becomes red, 3–4 minutes. Set aside.

Place dried shrimp in a food processor and process until fine, 2–3 minutes. Add remaining ingredients, except chicken stock, and process to a smooth paste, about 3 minutes.

Return chili oil to heat and add paste. Cook, stirring, until oil comes to surface, 3–4 minutes. Add chicken stock and bring mixture to a steady simmer. Simmer for 15 minutes. Strain mixture through a fine sieve and set aside. Discard solids.

To make soup: Heat peanut oil in a large saucepan over medium heat until hot, about 1 minute. Add onion and carrot. Cook, stirring, until just soft, 4–5 minutes. Add chicken, mushrooms and tom yum stock and bring to a steady simmer. Add lime leaves and simmer until chicken is cooked through, about 10 minutes. Season to taste with lime juice and fish sauce, 1 teaspoon at a time. Remove lime leaves. Ladle into individual bowls and serve each bowl garnished with a basil sprig.

Serves 4

Malay chicken soup with rice

2 teaspoons light olive oil

1 yellow (brown) onion, sliced

3 stalks celery, cut into thin strips

2 medium carrots, peeled and sliced

1 whole chicken, about 4 lb (2 kg)

8 cups (64 fl oz/2 L) water

2 lemongrass stalks, bottom 3 inches (7.5 cm)
  only, chopped into 2-inch (5-cm) pieces

2-inch (5-cm) piece fresh galangal or fresh ginger,
  peeled and sliced

2 large sprigs cilantro (coriander), including
  roots

2 teaspoons sea salt

1/2 teaspoon white pepper

1 1/2 cups (11 oz/330 g) jasmine rice, rinsed until
  water runs clear

2 tablespoons finely chopped fresh chives

2 tablespoons crispy fried onions

soy sauce, for serving

chili sauce, for serving

Heat olive oil in a large saucepan (large enough to hold whole chicken) over medium–high heat. Add onion, celery and carrots and cook, stirring, until onions are soft, about 5 minutes. Place chicken on top of vegetables and add 8 cups (64 fl oz/2 L) water to completely cover chicken. Add lemongrass, galangal, cilantro, salt and pepper and bring liquid to a steady simmer. Reduce heat to medium–low and simmer for 1½ hours, occasionally skimming any oil and scum from surface.

Drain mixture, reserving chicken and stock and discarding other solids. Allow chicken to cool slightly, then chop, with a large, heavy knife or cleaver, into medium-sized sections (wings, quartered breasts, drumsticks and thighs). Return stock to a large saucepan and add rinsed rice. Bring stock to a boil over high heat. Boil until rice is cooked, about 15 minutes. Stir in chives.

Ladle soup and rice into individual bowls and place chicken on top. Sprinkle with crispy fried onions and serve immediately, accompanied by small bowls of soy sauce and chili sauce for each diner to add if desired.

Serves 4

Roast duck laksa with papaya and Chinese spinach

2 teaspoons light olive oil

$^1/_4$ cup (2 oz/60 g) laksa paste (see page 18 for recipe)

2 cups (16 fl oz/500 ml) coconut milk

4 cups (64 fl oz/1 L) chicken stock (see page 14 for step-by-step instructions)

3 tablespoons lime juice

1 tablespoon fish sauce

1 Chinese roast duck (meat from breast and thigh bones removed and chopped, legs intact)

1 bunch small Chinese spinach, bok choy or choy sum, trimmed, or 3$^1/_2$ oz (100 g) baby English spinach leaves

1 small papaya, peeled, seeded and cut into $^1/_2$-inch (12-mm) pieces

1 small cucumber, peeled and sliced

1 medium red (Spanish) onion, finely sliced

4 tablespoons crispy fried onions

8 small sprigs cilantro (coriander) or basil

Heat oil in a large saucepan over medium heat and add laksa paste. Cook, stirring, until paste is fragrant, 4–5 minutes. Add coconut milk, chicken stock, lime juice and fish sauce and cook for 15 minutes. Add more fish sauce for a saltier flavor.

Stir in duck and Chinese spinach and cook until duck is heated through and spinach is wilted, 2–3 minutes.

Ladle soup into individual bowls and top with papaya, cucumber, red onion, crispy fried onions and cilantro sprigs. Serve immediately.

Serves 4

Sweet potato and roast duck soup

2 medium sweet potatoes

1 tablespoon plus 2 teaspoons light olive oil

2 large red (Spanish) onions, very thinly sliced

3 cloves garlic, minced

2-inch (5-cm) piece fresh ginger, peeled and grated

8 cups (64 fl oz/2 L) chicken stock (see page 14 for step-by-step instructions)

2 small red chili peppers, thinly sliced

grated zest (rind) of 1 lime

1 Chinese roast duck, meat removed from bones

1 teaspoon fish sauce

2 tablespoons lime juice

freshly ground black pepper

1/2 cup (1/2 oz/15 g) cilantro (coriander) leaves plus 4 sprigs

1/2 cup (1/2 oz/15 g) small basil leaves

1/2 cup (1/2 oz/15 g) small mint leaves

Preheat oven to 400°F (200°C/Gas 6). Place sweet potatoes on an oven rack and bake until a skewer inserted through thickest part meets with no resistance, 30–40 minutes. Remove sweet potatoes from oven and set aside to cool. When cool enough to handle, remove skins and chop flesh into pieces.

Heat 1 tablespoon oil in a large saucepan over medium heat. Add half the onion slices, half the garlic and half the ginger and cook, stirring, for 3–4 minutes. Add chicken stock and bring liquid to a steady simmer. Simmer for 15 minutes. Reduce heat to medium–low and add chopped sweet potato. Cook for 2–3 minutes, then remove from heat and allow to cool slightly. Place mixture, working in batches, in a food processor and purée until smooth, about 3 minutes. Return puréed mixture to large saucepan and keep hot enough to serve.

Heat remaining oil in a large frying pan or wok. Add remaining onion, chili peppers, remaining garlic and ginger, lime zest and duck and cook, tossing and stirring, for 1 minute. Remove from heat and add fish sauce, lime juice, black pepper, cilantro, basil and mint. Stir until combined.

Ladle soup into individual bowls, top with the duck mixture and serve immediately.

Serves 4

SWEET POTATO AND ROAST DUCK SOUP

Hanoi chicken soup

2 cloves garlic, crushed

2 tablespoons soy sauce

2 boneless, skinless chicken breasts, 6 oz (180 g) each

6 oz (180 g) dried rice noodles

8 cups (64 fl oz/2 L) pho chicken stock (see page 19 for recipe)

4 scallions (shallots/spring onions), green and white parts, cut into strips

1 cup (1 oz/30 g) basil leaves, preferably purple or Thai

1/2 cup (1/2 oz/15 g) small mint leaves

7 oz (220 g) bean sprouts, watercress or snow pea shoots, trimmed

2 tablespoons prepared chili paste or sambal oelek

Combine garlic, soy sauce and ½ cup (4 fl oz/125 ml) water in a large saucepan, with a lid, that can accommodate a bamboo steamer and its lid. Place over high heat and bring to a boil. Reduce heat to medium so liquid is at a steady simmer.

Line bottom of a bamboo steamer with two pieces of wax paper cut to approximate size of each chicken breast. Place chicken breasts on wax paper in steamer, then set steamer inside saucepan. Cover steamer and saucepan and steam chicken until cooked through, 12–15 minutes (test by cutting through thickest part with a small, sharp knife). Check steaming liquid occasionally and add more water if necessary. Remove cooked chicken and set aside.

Place noodles in a large bowl and add boiling water to cover. Allow noodles to stand until soft, 3–4 minutes. Drain and set aside in colander.

In a large saucepan, heat pho stock over a high heat until boiling.

Slice cooked chicken into thin strips.

Quickly rinse noodles under very hot water, using a fork to separate them. Place noodles in individual bowls and top with chicken. Pour stock into bowls. Serve remaining ingredients in small bowls for diners to add to soup.

Serves 4

Chinese hot-and-sour soup

8 cups (64 fl oz/2 L) chicken stock (see page 14 for step-by-step instructions)

2 oz (60 g) dried vermicelli noodles, broken into pieces about 1–2 inches (2.5–5 cm)

4 dried shiitake mushrooms

7 oz (220 g) finely diced skinless, boneless chicken from breast or thigh

1/2 cup (4 oz/125 g) canned bamboo shoots

1 teaspoon peeled and finely grated fresh ginger

2 tablespoons ketchup (tomato sauce) or 1 tablespoon tomato paste

1 tablespoon sherry vinegar

1/2 teaspoon ground white pepper

2 scallions (shallots/spring onions), finely sliced

1 small red chili pepper, finely chopped

Heat stock in large saucepan over medium heat. Place noodles in a bowl, add boiling water to cover and soak until soft, 3–5 minutes.

Drain and add to the stock. Place dried mushrooms in a bowl, add boiling water to cover and soak for 5 minutes. Drain, slice thinly and add to stock. Add diced chicken, bamboo shoots and ginger and stir to combine. Cook until chicken is tender, 3–4 minutes. Stir in remaining ingredients and cook for 1–2 minutes. Taste and adjust seasonings by adding a little more vinegar or chili as desired. Serve immediately, ladled into bowls.

Serves 4

Hot and sour shrimp soup

1 lb (500 g) green shrimp (prawns), peeled, heads and shells reserved

1 medium white onion, chopped

2 stalks lemongrass, bottom 3 inches (7.5 cm) only, cut into 1-inch (2.5-cm) lengths

4 fresh or 8 dried kaffir lime leaves

1 tablespoon fish sauce

3 tablespoons lime juice

1 long red chili pepper, thinly sliced

1 small red (Spanish) onion, thinly sliced

1 large carrot, peeled and sliced into rounds or flowers*

8 large sprigs cilantro (coriander), for garnish

Place shrimp heads and shells in a large saucepan with 8 cups (64 fl oz/2 L) water. Add white onion, half the lemongrass and half the kaffir lime leaves. Bring mixture to a boil over high heat then reduce heat to medium and simmer for 25 minutes. Strain mixture through a fine sieve and discard solids. Pour stock into a large saucepan and add remaining lemongrass and kaffir lime leaves, fish sauce, lime juice, chili pepper, red onion and carrot. Simmer over medium heat until carrots are tender, about 10 minutes. Add shrimp and simmer until cooked through, 3–4 minutes. Adjust seasonings by adding more fish sauce if soup is not salty enough or more lime juice if it is not tangy enough.

Remove kaffir lime leaves and ladle soup into individual bowls. Serve immediately, topped with cilantro sprigs.

* Cut carrots into slices ⅛ inch (3 mm) thick. Make flowers using small, flower-shaped cookie (pastry) cutter.

Serves 4

HOT AND SOUR SHRIMP SOUP

Marinated lime-and-chili fish soup

1/2 lb (250 g) white-fleshed fish fillet

2 teaspoons chili oil

1 small red chili pepper, finely chopped

2 cloves garlic, crushed

2-inch (5-cm) piece fresh ginger, peeled and
   finely grated

1 medium red (Spanish) onion, very finely sliced

1/2 teaspoon white pepper

3 tablespoons lime juice

2 teaspoons fish sauce

3 medium tomatoes, cored and chopped into
   3/4-inch (2-cm) pieces

6 oz (180 g) thin rice noodles

6 cups (48 fl oz/1.5 L) fish stock (see page 16 for
   recipe)

4 sprigs cilantro (coriander), for garnish

Remove skin and any bones from fish fillet and cut fish diagonally, across grain, into very thin slices. Place in a large glass or ceramic bowl and add chili oil, chili pepper, garlic, ginger, onion, white pepper, lime juice, fish sauce and tomatoes. Stir very gently to coat fish with marinade. Cover with plastic wrap and refrigerate for 2–3 hours.

Place noodles in a bowl and add boiling water to cover. Let noodles stand until soft, 3–4 minutes. Drain noodles, rinse under warm water and set aside.

When ready to serve, rinse noodles under very hot water, using a fork to separate them. Drain and divide among bowls. Spoon fish mixture over noodles. Bring stock to a boil over high heat. Immediately pour into bowls so ingredients are completely covered. Let soup stand until fish is cooked, 3–4 minutes. Serve garnished with cilantro sprigs.

Serves 4

MARINATED LIME-AND-CHILI FISH SOUP

Miso soup with tuna and ginger

$^1\!/_4$ cup (2 oz/60 g) miso paste

6 cups (48 fl oz/1.5 L) light fish stock or water

2-inch (5-cm) piece fresh ginger, peeled and thinly sliced

4 scallions (shallots/spring onions), white part only, cut into thin strips

6 oz (180 g) soft tofu, cut into $^1\!/_2$-inch (12-mm) cubes

2 tablespoons shredded seaweed

8 oz (250 g) sashimi-quality tuna

1 tablespoon wasabi powder

$^1\!/_4$ cup (1$^1\!/_2$ fl oz/45 g) Japanese pickled ginger

Place miso paste in a large saucepan with fish stock and ginger and stir over medium heat until liquid reaches a steady simmer and miso paste is completely dissolved, about 10 minutes. Reduce heat to low and add scallions, tofu and seaweed. Simmer for 3 minutes.

Meanwhile, slice tuna into very thin strips. Prepare wasabi paste by mixing wasabi powder with 2 teaspoons water (or enough to form a thick paste) and stirring until smooth.

Pour miso soup into individual bowls and accompany with sliced tuna, wasabi paste and pickled ginger. Dip tuna in hot soup to cook it slightly, then eat soup and tuna with wasabi and pickled ginger. Serve with spoons or sip soup directly from bowls.

Serves 4

MISO SOUP WITH TUNA AND GINGER

Mussels in spiced coconut milk broth

1 large yellow (brown) onion, sliced

3 cloves garlic

1 teaspoon ground coriander

1/4 teaspoon turmeric

2 small red chili peppers

1 stalk lemongrass, bottom 3 inches (7.5 cm) only, chopped

2 tablespoons lemon juice

1 tablespoon light olive oil

2 cups (16 fl oz/500 ml) fish stock (see page 16 for recipe)

2 cups (16 fl oz/500 ml) coconut milk

2 teaspoons fish sauce

4 lb (2 kg) mussels in their shells, scrubbed

2-inch (5-cm) piece fresh ginger, very finely sliced lengthwise and julienned

1/2 cup (1/2 oz/15 g) cilantro (coriander) leaves

Combine onion, garlic, coriander, turmeric, chili peppers, lemongrass and lemon juice in a food processor and process mixture to a fine paste, 2–3 minutes.

Heat oil in a very large saucepan, with a lid, over medium heat and add paste. Cook, stirring, until fragrant, about 5 minutes. Add fish stock, coconut milk and fish sauce, increase heat to high and bring liquid to a boil. Add mussels, then cover saucepan tightly and cook, shaking saucepan occasionally, until all mussels have opened, 7–8 minutes. Discard any mussels that did not open. Add ginger and cilantro and stir to combine thoroughly.

Serve immediately in large bowls.

Serves 4

Octopus and squid laksa

1 tablespoon Asian sesame oil

3 tablespoons fish sauce

5 tablespoons (3 fl oz/80 ml) lime juice

1 tablespoon honey

2 small red chili peppers, finely chopped

1/4 cup (1/4 oz/7 g) finely chopped fresh cilantro (coriander)

2 tablespoons finely chopped fresh mint

8 oz (250 g) baby octopus, trimmed of head and beak

8 oz (250 g) small whole squid, cleaned, trimmed and cut into rings
  1/2 inch (12 mm) thick

1 tablespoon peanut oil

1 medium yellow (brown) onion, chopped

2 tablespoons grated fresh ginger

2 teaspoons crushed garlic

1 tablespoon chili paste or sambal oelek

1 teaspoon ground coriander

1/4 teaspoon turmeric

2 cups (16 fl oz/500 ml) coconut milk

4 cups (32 fl oz/1 L) fish stock (see page 16 for recipe)

8 oz (250 g) deep-fried tofu

4 sprigs mint

4 sprigs basil

1 small red (Spanish) onion, very thinly sliced

1 small cucumber, sliced and julienned

1 red chili pepper (optional), sliced

1/4 cup (2 oz/60 g) crispy fried onions or shallots (French shallots) (see
  page 58 for recipe)

Combine sesame oil, 2 tablespoons fish sauce, 2 tablespoons lime juice, honey, chili peppers, cilantro and mint in a glass or ceramic bowl. Add squid and octopus, then cover and refrigerate. Allow to marinate for 3 hours.

Heat peanut oil in a large saucepan over medium–high heat. Add onion, ginger, garlic, chili paste, ground coriander and turmeric and cook, stirring, until onion is soft and mixture is fragrant, about 5 minutes. Add remaining lime juice, coconut milk, fish stock and remaining fish sauce. Bring liquid to a boil, then reduce heat to medium–low and simmer for 15–20 minutes.

Preheat broiler (grill). Remove squid and octopus from marinade and discard marinade. Grill squid and octopus until cooked through and tender, 3–4 minutes for squid, 4–5 minutes for octopus.

Add squid and octopus to simmering soup and stir to combine. Ladle into individual bowls and pile high with remaining ingredients, finishing with crispy fried onions.

Serves 4

Penang laksa

2 tablespoons peanut oil

1 medium yellow (brown) onion, sliced

2 tablespoons laksa paste (see page 18 for recipe)

8 cups (64 fl oz/2 L) fish stock (see page 16 for recipe)

1/4 cup (2 fl oz/60 ml) lime or lemon juice

7 oz (220 g) dried rice noodles

1 lb (500 g) firm white-fleshed fish fillets, skin and bones removed, cut into 8 pieces

8 oz (250 g) scallops or shrimp (prawns)

4 deep-fried tofu pillows, halved

5 oz (150 g) bean sprouts, trimmed

4 quail eggs, hard boiled, peeled and halved (or 2 hard boiled chicken eggs, peeled and quartered)

4 small sprigs mint

4 small sprigs basil

1/4 cup crispy fried onions

Heat oil in a large saucepan over medium heat. Add onion and cook until it begins to soften, 3–4 minutes. Add laksa paste and continue to cook, stirring, until onion is soft and paste is fragrant, about 4 minutes. Add fish stock and lime juice, increase heat to medium–high and bring liquid to a steady simmer. Reduce heat to medium–low and simmer for 10 minutes.

Meanwhile, place noodles in a large bowl and add boiling water to cover. Allow to stand until noodles are soft, 3–5 minutes. Drain, rinse noodles in very hot water and set aside.

Add fish to laksa broth and simmer until cooked through, 4–5 minutes. Add scallops and tofu and cook for 1 minute.

Rinse noodles under very hot water, using a fork to keep them separate.

Spoon noodles into individual bowls and ladle soup over top, piling fish and scallops in middle. Top with remaining ingredients, finishing with crispy fried onions. Serve immediately.

Serves 4

PENANG LAKSA

Soup with salmon balls and Chinese spinach

1 lb (500 g) salmon fillet, skin and any bones removed, cut into
1-inch (2.5-cm) pieces

4 scallions (shallots/spring onions), green and white parts,
finely chopped

1 tablespoon finely chopped fresh ginger

2 cloves garlic, minced

1 small red chili pepper, finely chopped

1/2 teaspoon white pepper

1/2 teaspoon sea salt

2 teaspoons finely grated lime zest (rind)

2 tablespoons finely chopped fresh cilantro (coriander)

1 large egg white, lightly beaten

9 cups (72 fl oz/1.25 L) fish stock (see page 16 for recipe)

1 tablespoon light olive oil

1 large red (Spanish) onion, sliced

2-inch (5-cm) piece fresh ginger, peeled and thinly sliced

1 large carrot, peeled and julienned

2 tablespoons lime juice

sea salt and ground white pepper

1/2 lb (250 g) Chinese spinach, bok choy, choy sum or baby
English spinach, trimmed

Place salmon pieces in a food processor and process until fish is minced and forms a mass when a small amount is shaped, about 2 minutes. Place salmon in a bowl with scallions, ginger, garlic, chili pepper, white pepper, salt, lime zest, cilantro and egg white. Mix until thoroughly combined. Line a sheet of parchment (baking paper) with waxed paper. Take a large teaspoonful of mixture and form it into a ball. Place on waxed paper. Repeat with remaining mixture.

Heat 1 cup (8 fl oz/250 ml) fish stock with 1 cup (8 fl oz/ 250 ml) water in a saucepan over medium–low heat. Bring mixture to a slow simmer. Add fish balls, 5 at a time, and simmer until just cooked through, about 4 minutes. Remove with a slotted spoon and set aside. Cover fish balls loosely with plastic wrap so they do not dry out. Repeat with remaining fish balls.

Heat oil in a large saucepan over medium heat and add onion and ginger slices. Cook until onion begins to soften, 3–4 minutes. Add carrot pieces and cook for 2 minutes. Add remaining stock and lime juice and bring mixture to a steady simmer. Simmer for 15 minutes. Season to taste with salt and white pepper. Add spinach and fish balls and simmer until fish balls have heated through and spinach is wilted, about 3 minutes.

Serve immediately, ladled into large bowls.

Serves 4

SOUP WITH SALMON BALLS AND CHINESE SPINACH

Poached salmon
and green bean soup

1 tablespoon light olive oil

1 medium yellow (brown) onion, finely diced

1 small red chili pepper, minced

3 lemongrass stalks, bottom 3 inches (7.5 cm)
 only, cut lengthwise in half

4 fresh or 8 dried kaffir lime leaves

3 cups (24 fl oz/750 ml) fish stock (see page 16
 for recipe)

3 cups (24 fl oz/750 ml) coconut milk

3 tablespoons lime juice

2 teaspoons fish sauce

freshly ground black or white pepper to taste

1 lb (500 g) salmon fillet, skin and any bones
 removed, cut into 1-inch (2.5-cm) pieces

10 oz (310 g) peeled fava (broad) beans

8 oz (250 g) baby green beans, trimmed, halved
 if large

Heat oil in a large saucepan over medium heat. Add onion and chili pepper and cook, stirring, until onion is soft, 4–5 minutes. Add lemongrass, kaffir lime leaves, fish stock, coconut milk, lime juice, fish sauce and ground pepper. Bring liquid to a steady simmer. Simmer for 15 minutes. Reduce heat to medium–low and add salmon. Cook for 2 minutes, then add fava and green beans and cook until beans are just tender and salmon is just cooked through, 3–4 minutes. Add more fish sauce if soup is not salty enough or more lime juice if it is not tangy enough.

Serve in individual small bowls.

Serves 4

Hint

Soup may be served with jasmine rice.

POACHED SALMON AND GREEN BEAN SOUP

Seafood laksa

FOR LAKSA

1½ tablespoons light olive oil

½ cup (4 oz/125 g) laksa paste (see page 18 for recipe)

2 tablespoons lime or lemon juice

3 cups (24 fl oz/750 ml) coconut milk

3 cups (24 fl oz/750 ml) fish stock (see page 16 for recipe)

6 oz (180 g) dried rice vermicelli noodles

12 oz (375 g) medium shrimp (prawns), peeled and deveined, tails left intact

16 oz (500 g) salmon fillet, cut into 8 pieces 1 inch (5 cm) thick

1 medium red (Spanish) onion, thinly sliced

1 medium cucumber, peeled and sliced

7 oz (220 g) bean sprouts, trimmed

5 oz (150 g) mustard cress shoots or snowpea shoots

1 medium mango, 12 oz (375 g), peeled, seeded and diced

2 tablespoons small mint leaves

¼ cup (2 oz/60 g) crispy fried shallots (French shallots) (see recipe below)

FOR CRISPY FRIED SHALLOTS (FRENCH SHALLOTS)

2 cups (16 fl oz/500 ml) peanut oil

5 or 6 medium shallots (French shallots), about 5 oz (150 g), peeled and very thinly sliced

To make laksa: Heat oil in a large saucepan over medium–high heat. Stir in laksa paste and cook, stirring, until fragrant, 4–5 minutes. Add lime juice, coconut milk and stock and stir until thoroughly combined. Reduce heat to medium and simmer for 10 minutes.

Place noodles in a large bowl and add boiling water to cover. Let stand until noodles are soft, 3–4 minutes. Drain noodles, rinse under warm water and set aside.

Add shrimp and salmon to soup and simmer until shrimp are cooked through and salmon is just cooked through, 3–4 minutes.

Rinse noodles under very hot water, using a fork to separate them.

Spoon noodles into individual bowls and top with soup and seafood. Top with remaining ingredients, finishing with crispy fried shallots. Serve immediately.

Serves 4

To make crispy fried shallots: Heat oil in a medium saucepan over high heat until it reaches 375°F (190°C) on a deep-frying thermometer. Add shallots all at once and fry until golden, about 1½ minutes. Remove with a slotted spoon and drain on a plate lined with paper towels.

Makes 1 cup/8 oz/250 g

Shrimp, noodle and herb soup

2 lb (1 kg) shrimp (prawns), peeled, heads and
shells reserved

2 tablespoons soy sauce

2 tablespoons lemon juice

1 large yellow (brown) onion, chopped

2-inch (5-cm) piece fresh ginger, peeled and
sliced

4 fresh or 8 dried kaffir lime leaves

2 stalks lemongrass, cut lengthwise into 3 inch
(7.5 cm) lengths each, or 4 strips lemon zest
(rind)

sea salt to taste

8 oz (250 g) fresh egg noodles

1/2 cup (1/2 oz/15 g) cilantro (coriander) leaves

1/2 cup (1/2 oz/15 g) small basil leaves

4 cups (8 oz/250 g) chopped Chinese greens, such
as bok choy, choy sum or English spinach

4 scallions (shallots/spring onions), thinly sliced,
for garnish

Place shrimp in a glass or ceramic bowl and stir in soy sauce and lemon juice. Cover and refrigerate for at least 30 minutes. Place shrimp heads and shells in a large saucepan with onion, ginger, kaffir lime leaves and lemongrass. Add 8 cups (64 fl oz/2 L) water, place over medium–high heat and bring to a steady simmer. Simmer for 25 minutes. Add salt to taste. Strain and reserve broth. Discard solids.

Bring a large pot of water to a boil. Add noodles and cook until soft and cooked through, 5–7 minutes. Drain, rinse under very hot water and set aside.

Skim shrimp stock of any residue on surface and place in a large saucepan over medium–high heat. Bring to a steady simmer, then add noodles and shrimp and marinade. Reduce heat to low and simmer until heated through, about 1 minute. Add herbs and chopped greens and simmer until greens have wilted, about 1 minute.

Ladle into individual bowls and serve topped with sliced scallions.

Serves 4

SHRIMP. NOODLE AND HERB SOUP

Sour crabmeat soup

1 tablespoon light olive oil

2 medium red (Spanish) onions, sliced

2-inch (5-cm) piece fresh ginger, peeled and sliced

4 cloves garlic, peeled and crushed

2 stalks lemongrass, bottom 3 inches (7.5 cm)
  only, cut lengthwise into strips

1 small red chili pepper, finely chopped

3 tablespoons lime juice

3 fresh or 6 dried kaffir lime leaves

8 cups (64 fl oz/2 L) fish stock (see page 16 for
  recipe)

2 teaspoons fish sauce

1 lb (500 g) prepared crabmeat (picked from shells)

1 small red (Spanish) onion, very thinly sliced, for
  garnish

1 red chili pepper, sliced crosswise, for garnish

Heat oil in a large saucepan over medium–high heat. Add onions and cook until onions begin to soften, about 3 minutes. Add ginger, garlic, lemongrass and chili pepper and cook, stirring, until mixture is fragrant, about 3 minutes. Add lime juice, kaffir lime leaves, stock and fish sauce and bring mixture to a steady simmer. Simmer for 20 minutes.

Strain mixture through a fine sieve, discarding solids, and return liquid to saucepan. Heat over medium heat until it simmers, 2–3 minutes. Add crabmeat and simmer until heated through, 2–3 minutes.

Pour into individual bowls and serve immediately, garnished with slices of onion and chili pepper.

Serves 4

SOUR CRABMEAT SOUP

beef

Beef and cabbage soup

1 red chili pepper

4 shallots (French shallots), peeled

2 cloves garlic, peeled

1 teaspoon galangal powder or 1 tablespoon chopped fresh galangal or fresh ginger

1/2 cup (1/2 oz/15 g) cilantro (coriander) leaves

2 tablespoons finely grated lime zest (rind)

1 teaspoon coriander seeds

1 teaspoon cumin seeds

5 black peppercorns

1 teaspoon paprika

1/4 teaspoon turmeric

1/4 cup (2 fl oz/ 60 ml) light olive oil

1 medium yellow (brown) onion, chopped

1 lb (500 g) blade, round or chuck steak, cut into 1-inch (2.5-cm) cubes

6 cups (48 fl oz/1.5 L) pho beef stock (see page 19 for recipe)

2 cups (16 fl oz/500 ml) coconut milk

4 medium, ripe tomatoes, chopped

2 teaspoons fish sauce

3 cups (9 oz/280 g) shredded white or Chinese cabbage

Combine chili pepper, shallots, garlic, galangal, cilantro, lime zest, coriander seeds, cumin seeds, peppercorns, paprika, turmeric and oil in a food processor and process to a smooth paste, about 2 minutes. Place paste in a large saucepan over medium–low heat and cook, stirring, for 5 minutes. Add a little more oil if mixture starts to stick to bottom of pan. Add onion and meat and cook, stirring, until onion is soft and meat is slightly browned, about 5 minutes. Add stock, coconut milk, tomatoes and fish sauce, increase heat to medium and bring mixture to a steady simmer. Simmer until meat is tender, about 1½ hours. Stir in cabbage and cook until the cabbage is soft, about 10 minutes.

Ladle into individual bowls and serve.

Serves 4

BEEF AND CABBAGE SOUP

Beef soup with coconut milk and Thai herbs

2 cloves garlic

2 tablespoons peeled and finely chopped fresh ginger

3 shallots (French shallots), peeled

1 teaspoon galangal powder

1/2 teaspoons sea salt

1/2 teaspoon white peppercorns

4 cilantro (coriander) roots

1 small red chili pepper

3 tablespoons light olive oil

12 oz (375 g) round or rump steak, cut into 1-inch (2.5-cm) cubes

5 cups (40 fl oz/1.25 L) coconut milk

3 cups (24 fl oz/750 ml) pho beef stock (see page 19 for recipe)

2–3 tablespoons lemon juice

2 stalks lemongrass, bottom 4 inches (10 cm) only, cut into 2-inch (5-cm) pieces

3 fresh or 6 dried kaffir lime leaves

2 teaspoons palm sugar or dark brown sugar

1 tablespoon fish sauce

6 1/2 oz (200 g) baby English spinach leaves

Combine garlic, ginger, shallots, galangal, salt, peppercorns, cilantro, chili pepper and 2 tablespoons oil in a food processor and process to a smooth paste, 1–2 minutes.

Heat remaining oil in a large saucepan over medium heat. Add paste and cook, stirring, until fragrant, 3–4 minutes. Add meat and cook for 3–4 minutes, turning to coat meat and brown it slightly. Add coconut milk, stock and lemon juice and bring mixture to a steady simmer. Add lemongrass, kaffir lime leaves, palm sugar, and fish sauce and simmer until meat is tender, about 30 minutes. Remove lemongrass and lime leaves. Season to taste with fish sauce if soup is not salty enough and lemon juice if it is not tangy enough.

Stir in spinach leaves and let soup stand until leaves are wilted, about 1 minute. Serve immediately.

Serves 4

BEEF SOUP WITH COCONUT MILK AND THAI HERBS

Beef with ginger and asparagus soup

¹/₄ cup (2 oz/60 g) miso paste

6 cups (48 fl oz/1.5 L) light beef stock or water

2-inch (5-cm) piece fresh ginger, peeled and cut into thin strips

4 very small red (Spanish) onions, peeled and halved, or 4 pearl onions

13 oz (400 g) beef fillet, cut into very thin slices

8 asparagus spears, thinly sliced crosswise

1 cup (3 oz/90 g) very thinly sliced red cabbage

Place miso paste in a large saucepan with stock. Stir over medium–high heat until miso paste dissolves, 2–3 minutes. Allow liquid to come to a steady simmer. Add ginger (reserving a small amount for garnish) and onions and simmer for 10 minutes. Add beef, asparagus and red cabbage and simmer until asparagus and cabbage are tender, 1–2 minutes.

Serve immediately, garnished with reserved ginger strips.

Serves 4

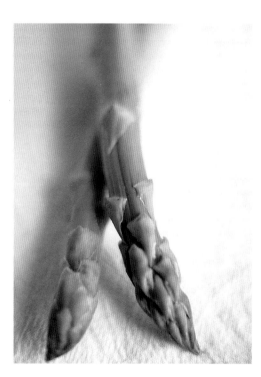

Variation

Instead of asparagus, use baby English spinach or finely sliced snow peas (mange-tout). If you prefer a chili flavor, add chili sauce to taste.

BEEF WITH GINGER AND ASPARAGUS SOUP

Pho with meatballs

1¹/₂ lb (750 g) ground (minced) beef

¹/₄ cup (¹/₃ oz/10 g) finely chopped fresh cilantro
(coriander)

¹/₄ cup (¹/₃ oz/10 g) finely chopped fresh basil
leaves

¹/₄ cup (¹/₃ oz/10 g) finely chopped fresh parsley

2 cloves garlic, minced

¹/₂ teaspoon white pepper

1 teaspoon sea salt

5 oz (150 g) fresh rice noodles

9 cups (72 fl oz/2.25 L) pho beef stock (see page
19 for recipe)

2 tablespoons lime juice

4 oz (125 g) baby spinach leaves, for serving

3 oz (90 g) bean sprouts, for serving

lime wedges, for serving

chili paste, for serving

In a bowl, combine ground beef with herbs, garlic, white pepper and salt. Stir thoroughly to combine. Take a large teaspoonful of mixture and form it into a ball. Place on a baking sheet. Repeat with remaining ingredients. Cover loosely with plastic wrap and refrigerate until ready to cook.

Bring a large saucepan of water to a boil. Add rice noodles and cook until soft, 3–4 minutes. Drain and set aside.

Heat 1 cup (8 fl oz/250 ml) stock in a saucepan over medium–low heat and bring to a steady simmer. Add meatballs, 5 or 6 at a time, and cook, turning, until cooked through, about 4 minutes. Set aside. Skim stock and place in a large saucepan with remaining stock and lime juice. Place over medium heat and bring to a steady simmer. Add meatballs and cook until heated through, about 1 minute.

Rinse noodles under very hot water, using a fork to separate them. Place in individual bowls. Ladle soup and meatballs over noodles. Serve with remaining ingredients in small bowls for each diner to add according to taste.

Serves 4

Chinese smoked ham and black-eyed pea soup

1½ cups (10 oz/300 g) black-eyed peas (beans)

1 tablespoon light olive oil

10 shallots (French shallots), finely sliced

2-inch (5-cm) piece fresh ginger, peeled and
   coarsely grated

2 cloves garlic, chopped

1 teaspoon Chinese five spice powder

2 tablespoons dry sherry

1 tablespoons soy sauce

2 tablespoons honey

1 smoked ham bone* or 2 cups (1 lb/500 g)
   shredded cooked smoked ham

8 cups (64 fl oz/2 L) chicken or vegetable stock
   (see page 14 for step-by-step chicken stock)

2 cups (16 fl oz/500 ml) water

2 tablespoons finely chopped fresh parsley

Place peas in a large bowl and cover with 5 cups (40 fl oz/1.25 L) water. Allow to soak for at least 3 hours, preferably overnight. Drain and set aside.

Heat oil in a large saucepan over medium heat. Add shallots, ginger, garlic and five spice powder and cook, stirring, until shallots are soft and slightly golden, about 5 minutes. Add sherry, soy sauce and honey and stir to combine. Add ham bone, stock and water, and stir to combine. Stir in peas. Bring liquid to a steady simmer and cook until peas are tender, about 45 minutes. If liquid level drops below peas, add more stock or water. Remove ham bone and cut off any remaining ham. Return ham to soup. Reheat soup and stir in parsley.

Ladle into large bowls and serve immediately.

* Ham bones are available at most meat markets and delicatessens. They usually have some ham left on the bone.

Serves 4

Classic beef pho

12 oz (375 g) lean beef fillet

10 oz (300 g) fresh thick rice noodles

6 oz (180 g) small green beans, trimmed

6 oz (180 g) snow peas (mange-tout), trimmed

1 small bunch cilantro (coriander), separated into

sprigs

1 cup (1 oz/30 g) small basil leaves

5 oz (150 g) bean sprouts, trimmed

8 cups (64 fl oz/2 L) pho beef stock (see page 19

for recipe)

1 lime, quartered

chili paste or sambal oelek, to taste

2 tablespoons fish sauce (optional), to taste

Wrap beef fillet in plastic wrap and freeze until it is firm and beginning to freeze completely, about 1 hour. Remove from freezer and slice as thinly as possible. Set aside at room temperature and allow to defrost completely.

Bring a large pot of water to a boil and add rice noodles. Cook until noodles are tender, 3–4 minutes. Drain noodles and place in a colander.

Bring a small saucepan with 1 inch (2.5 cm) water to a boil. Add green beans and snow peas and cook for 1 minute. Drain immediately and place in a bowl with cilantro, basil and bean sprouts. Set aside.

Heat stock in a saucepan until boiling. Rinse noodles under very hot water quickly, using a fork to separate them. Divide among 4 bowls. Pour stock over noodles and top with beef slices.

Allow to stand for 1–2 minutes. Top with herbs and vegetables. Add a squeeze of lime, and chili sauce and fish sauce to taste.

Serves 4

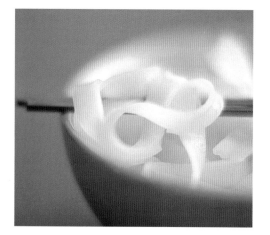

Combination soup

3 dried shiitake mushrooms

3¹/₂ oz (105 g) thin, dried rice noodles

1 tablespoon light olive oil

¹/₄ cup (¹/₃ oz/10 g) finely chopped fresh cilantro
(coriander)

¹/₂ teaspoon ground white pepper

2 cloves garlic, finely chopped

3 oz (90 g) pork fillet, trimmed of fat and sinew,
thinly sliced

6 oz (180 g) skinless, boneless chicken breast,
thinly sliced

8 cups (64 fl oz/2 L) chicken stock (see page 14
for step-by-step instructions)

1 tablespoon fish sauce

6 oz (180 g) medium shrimp (prawns), peeled and
deveined

¹/₄ cup (³/₄ oz/25 g) chopped scallions
(shallots/spring onions)

1 egg, lightly beaten

1 small cucumber, sliced, for garnish

Soak dried mushrooms in a small bowl of hot water for 30 minutes. Remove from water, cut off and discard stems and slice caps. Set aside.

Pour boiling water over noodles in a bowl and allow to stand until soft, 7–8 minutes. Drain and set aside.

Heat oil in a large saucepan over medium heat. Add cilantro, white pepper, garlic, pork, chicken and mushrooms and cook, stirring, for 3 minutes. Add stock and fish sauce and bring liquid to a steady simmer. Simmer for 15 minutes. Stir in shrimp and scallions and cook until shrimp are cooked through, 2–3 minutes. Increase heat to high and bring liquid to a boil. As soon as it boils, briskly stir in egg. Liquid must be boiling or egg will not set.

Rinse noodles under very hot water, using a fork to separate them, then spoon into individual bowls. Ladle soup over noodles and serve topped with cucumber.

Serves 4

COMBINATION SOUP

Japanese pork and spinach noodle soup

1 tablespoon light olive oil

1¹/₂ lb (750 g) pork fillet, trimmed of fat and
  sinew

2 tablespoons soy sauce

¹/₂ teaspoon ground white pepper, or to taste

¹/₄ cup (2 oz/60 g) miso paste

8 cups (64 fl oz/2 L) water

1 lb (500 g) fresh thick egg noodles

6 oz (180 g) baby English spinach leaves

2-inch (5-cm) piece fresh ginger, peeled and
  julienned

1 small red (Spanish) onion, cut into very thin
  slices

Heat oil in a large cast-iron frying pan over medium–high heat. Add pork and cook, turning, until well browned, 8–10 minutes. Test to see that middle is cooked to desired doneness by slicing into thickest part with tip of a sharp knife. Add soy sauce and season with white pepper. Remove from pan and set aside.

Place miso paste and water in a large saucepan over medium–high heat and cook, stirring, until miso paste is dissolved, 4–5 minutes. Reduce heat to low and simmer until ready to serve.

Bring a large saucepan filled with water to a boil. Add noodles and cook until tender, 5–7 minutes. Drain, then add noodles to miso soup. Add spinach and cook until wilted, about 1 minute. Cut pork into thin slices.

Ladle noodles and soup into large bowls and top with sliced pork, ginger and onion. Serve immediately.

Serves 4

JAPANESE PORK AND SPINACH NOODLE SOUP

Pork wonton, asparagus and noodle soup

1 lb (500 g) fresh, white, rice noodles

12 oz (375 g) ground (minced) pork

½ teaspoon white pepper

½ teaspoon sea salt

1 tablespoon peeled and grated fresh ginger

2 cloves garlic, crushed

1 green chili pepper, finely chopped

16 wonton wrappers

10 oz (300 g) asparagus, trimmed

2 tablespoons soy sauce

1 tablespoon lemon juice

1 tablespoon toasted sesame seeds

freshly ground black pepper

8 cups (64 fl oz/2 L) chicken stock (see page 14 for step-by-step instructions)

1 tablespoon finely chopped fresh cilantro (coriander), for garnish

Bring a large pot of water to a boil, stir in noodles and cook until tender, 3–4 minutes. Drain noodles, rinse in very hot water and set aside.

In a bowl, combine pork, white pepper, salt, ginger, garlic and chili pepper.

Lay wonton wrappers on a dry surface and place 1 heaping teaspoon pork mixture in middle of each wrapper. Wet edges with a little water, using a pastry brush or your finger, and fold edges in to form bundles, pressing edges together to secure filling.

Choose a large saucepan with a lid and a large steamer, also with a lid that will fit inside saucepan. Pour boiling water in saucepan to a depth of 1 inch (2.5 cm). Cut a piece of waxed paper (to fit bottom of steamer) and place in steamer. Arrange half the wontons on paper. Cover with the lid of the steamer and place inside the saucepan. Cover and steam until wontons are tender, about 4 minutes. Set wontons aside on a slightly damp plate and repeat with remaining wontons. Keep covered with plastic wrap. Check water level in saucepan occasionally and add more if necessary.

Remove waxed paper from steamer and place asparagus spears in steamer. Cover and steam asparagus until tender, about 3 minutes. Place asparagus on a plate and drizzle with soy sauce and lemon juice. Sprinkle with sesame seeds and black pepper to taste.

Place stock in a large pot and bring to a boil. Reduce heat to a steady simmer and add steamed wontons and cooked noodles. Simmer for 1 minute. Ladle into individual bowls and serve topped with asparagus and sprinkled with cilantro.

Serves 4

PORK WONTON. ASPARAGUS AND NOODLE SOUP

Marinated beef laksa

10 oz (300 g) lean beef fillet

3 tablespoons lime juice

3 tablespoons light olive oil

1 teaspoon chili oil

1 small red chili pepper, chopped

2 scallions (shallots/spring onions), white part
only, finely chopped

1 clove garlic, minced

2 tablespoons finely chopped fresh cilantro
(coriander)

1/4 cup (2 oz/60 g) laksa paste (see page 18 for
recipe)

4 cups (32 fl oz/1 L) beef or vegetable stock (see
page 19 for pho beef stock recipe)

4 cups (32 fl oz/1 L) coconut milk

2 teaspoons fish sauce

2 cups (4 oz/125 g) baby spinach leaves

4 oz (125 g) mixed fresh mushrooms (enoki, cremini,
shiitake and button), sliced if large, for garnish

4 oz (125 g) deep-fried tofu (about 4 pillows),
sliced, for garnish

4 large sprigs cilantro (coriander), for garnish

1/4 cup (2 oz/60 g) crispy fried onions or shallots
(French shallots), for garnish (see page 58 for
recipe)

Wrap beef fillet in plastic wrap and freeze until partially frozen, about 1 hour. Remove from freezer and slice into very thin strips. Place in a ceramic or glass bowl and add 1 tablespoon lime juice, 1 tablespoon olive oil, chili oil, chili pepper, scallions, garlic and cilantro. Mix gently to combine marinade ingredients. Cover and refrigerate for 1 hour.

Heat remaining oil in a large saucepan over medium–high heat until hot, about 1 minute. Add laksa paste and cook, stirring, until very fragrant, about 5 minutes. Add remaining lime juice, stock, coconut milk and fish sauce, reduce heat to medium and bring mixture to a steady simmer. Simmer for 15 minutes. Stir in spinach and simmer until leaves have wilted, about 1 minute.

Remove beef from refrigerator. Ladle soup into individual bowls and add beef and marinade. Top with garnishes, finishing with crispy fried onions. The beef and mushrooms will cook in the stock. Serve immediately.

Serves 4

MARINATED BEEF LAKSA

Udon noodle soup with sesame pork and mushrooms

7 oz (220 g) dried udon noodles

1 tablespoon peanut oil

2-inch (5-cm) piece fresh ginger, peeled and grated

2 small leeks, white part only, thinly sliced

1 clove garlic, finely chopped

3 oz (90 g) fresh shiitake mushrooms, sliced

5 oz (150 g) button mushrooms, sliced

1 tablespoon soy sauce

1 tablespoon rice wine

6 cups (48 fl oz/1.5 L) chicken or beef stock (see pages 14 and 19 for

recipes)

2 teaspoons Asian sesame oil

12 oz (375 g) pork fillet

sea salt and white pepper to taste

2 tablespoons finely chopped chives, for garnish

FRIED ENOKI MUSHROOMS

$^{1}/_{4}$ cup (2 oz/60 g) all-purpose (plain) flour

sea salt and freshly ground black pepper

$1^{1}/_{2}$ cups (12 fl oz/375 ml) peanut oil, for frying

4 bundles (2 oz/60 g) enoki mushrooms, divided into smaller bundles of

2 or 3 mushrooms

Bring a large pot of water to a boil. Add noodles and cook until tender, 7–9 minutes. Drain noodles, rinse with warm water and set aside.

Heat oil in a saucepan over medium–high heat and add ginger, leeks, garlic and mushrooms and cook, stirring, until leeks and mushrooms are wilted, 4–5 minutes. Add soy sauce, rice wine and stock, increase heat to high and bring liquid to a boil. Reduce heat to medium–low and simmer until ready to serve.

Heat sesame oil in a frying pan over high heat. Add pork fillet and cook, turning to brown all sides, 4–7 minutes. Reduce heat to medium and continue to cook until pork is cooked through (test by cutting into thickest part), 4–5 minutes. Season to taste with salt and white pepper. Remove pork from pan and set aside for 5 minutes.

To make fried enoki mushrooms: In a small bowl, combine flour with salt and black pepper to taste. Mix well. Heat oil in a large saucepan over high heat until a drop of flour sizzles rapidly when dropped in oil. Coat mushrooms in flour, shaking off excess. Fry mushrooms in hot oil until crisp and golden, about 40 seconds. Remove and drain on paper towels.

Cut pork into thin slices. Rinse noodles under very hot water, using a fork to separate them and place in individual bowls. Pour soup over noodles and top with pork slices and fried mushrooms. Sprinkle with chives and serve immediately.

Serves 4

Buddha's delight

4 oz (125 g) dried rice noodles

8 cups (64 fl oz/2 L) vegetable stock

2 cloves garlic, peeled and chopped

1 piece of fresh ginger, about 1 inch (2.5 cm), peeled and sliced

1 stalk lemongrass or zest (rind) of 1 lime, cut into 1-inch (3-cm) pieces

ground white pepper, to taste

1 tablespoon soy sauce, or to taste

1 tablespoon lime juice, or to taste

8 oz (250 g) butternut squash (pumpkin), cut into 1-inch (2.5-cm) cubes

4 oz (125 g) green beans

8 baby sweet corn cobs

1 carrot, peeled and julienned

1 bunch (13 oz/400 g) baby bok choy, leaves separated

1 green bell pepper (capsicum), seeded and sliced

4 oz (125 g) snow peas (mange-tout)

1 tomato, cut into 1-inch (2.5-cm) cubes

2 sprigs of fresh herbs, such as basil, cilantro (coriander) or chives

4 sprigs of mint, for garnish

chili paste or sambal oelek, for serving

Bring a large saucepan of water to a boil and add noodles. Remove from heat and allow to stand until soft, 4–5 minutes. Drain and divide among individual bowls.

Place stock in a large saucepan over medium–high heat, cover and bring to a boil. Add garlic, ginger, lemongrass, white pepper, soy sauce and lime juice, reduce heat to simmer and cook for about 1 minute. Add squash, beans, corn and carrot and cook until tender–crisp, about 2 minutes. Add bok choy, pepper, snow peas, tomato and herbs and cook until vegetables are tender, about 3 minutes.

Ladle soup over noodles and garnish with mint. Serve immediately with chili paste.

Serves 4

Chili corn soup

3 tablespoons light olive oil

2 red chili peppers

1 medium yellow (brown) onion

2 cloves garlic, peeled

1 teaspoon dried shrimp paste, optional

2 teaspoons finely grated lime zest (rind)

1 tablespoon chopped fresh ginger or fresh
    galangal or 2 teaspoons galangal powder

1 tablespoon coriander seeds

1 teaspoon cumin seeds

1/2 teaspoon fennel seeds

1/2 teaspoon ground cardamom

8 cups (64 fl oz/2 L) chicken or vegetable stock
    (see page 14 for step-by-step chicken stock)

4 cups (24 oz/750 g) fresh or frozen corn kernels

2 teaspoons fish sauce

1 tablespoon lime juice

1 roasted red bell pepper (capsicum), peeled and
    seeded

1 teaspoon chili paste or sambal oelek

Combine 2 tablespoons oil, chili peppers, onion, garlic, shrimp paste, lime zest, ginger and spices in a food processor and process to a smooth paste, 2–3 minutes.

Heat remaining oil in a large saucepan over medium heat and add paste. Cook, stirring, until fragrant, 3–4 minutes. Add stock, increase heat to medium–high and bring liquid to a steady simmer. Add corn, fish sauce and lime juice and simmer until corn is tender, about 5 minutes.

Let soup cool slightly. Working in batches if necessary, ladle into a food processor and process until smooth, 2–3 minutes. Return to saucepan and reheat before serving.

In a food processor, process bell pepper and chili paste until smooth, about 2 minutes.

Ladle soup into individual bowls and garnish with a little chili paste.

Serves 4

CHILI CORN SOUP

Japanese watercress soup

6 cups (48 fl oz/1.5 L) chicken or vegetable stock
(see page 14 for step-by-step chicken stock)

2 tablespoons soy sauce

2 eggs

4 cups (4 oz/125 g) watercress sprigs

white pepper to taste

soy sauce to taste, optional

Heat stock and soy sauce in a large saucepan over medium–high heat. Bring liquid to a steady simmer. Simmer for 3–4 minutes. Increase heat to high and bring liquid to a boil.

In a small bowl, using a fork, lightly whisk eggs then stir into soup. Keep stirring until eggs are set. Soup must be boiling for eggs to set.

Reduce heat to medium–low and add watercress. Simmer until watercress is wilted, about 2 minutes. Season to taste with white pepper and soy sauce if desired.

Ladle into individual bowls and serve immediately.

Serves 4

JAPANESE WATERCRESS SOUP

Miso ramen

¼ cup (2 oz/60 g) miso paste

2 tablespoons rice wine vinegar

6 cups (48 fl oz/1.5 L) vegetable stock or water

1 lb (500 g) fresh ramen noodles

2 tablespoons light olive oil

2 Asian eggplants (aubergines), about 4 oz (125 g)
each, cut crosswise into ½-inch (12-mm) slices

½ lb (250 g) mixed green leaf vegetables such as
baby English spinach, baby bok choy, Chinese
spinach and snow pea sprouts, chopped if large

4 oz (125 g) mushrooms, such as shiitake, button
or oyster varieties, chopped

5 scallions (shallots/spring onions), sliced, for
garnish

Combine miso paste, rice wine vinegar and stock in a large saucepan over medium–high heat. Cook, stirring, until miso paste is dissolved. Reduce heat to low and simmer gently while preparing the rest of the soup.

Bring a large pot of water to a boil, add noodles and cook until tender, 4–5 minutes. Drain noodles and set aside.

Heat oil in a frying pan over medium heat and cook eggplant slices on both sides until soft and golden, about 2 minutes per side. Set aside.

Add green leaf vegetables and mushrooms to simmering soup and cook until wilted and soft, 2–3 minutes.

Spoon noodles into individual bowls and ladle soup over noodles. Top with eggplant and scallions and serve immediately.

Serves 4

MISO RAMEN

Miso soup

¹/₄ cup (3 oz/90 g) soybean paste

5 oz (150 g) soft tofu, cut into 1-inch (2.5-cm) cubes

5 oz (150 g) button mushrooms, thinly sliced, optional

¹/₄ cup (¹/₃ oz/10 g) shredded dried seaweed

6¹/₂ oz (200 g) soft tofu, cut into ¹/₄-inch (6-mm) cubes

4 scallions (shallots/spring onions), white and green parts, thinly sliced on diagonal, for garnish

3 oz (90 g) snow pea sprouts, for garnish

Place soybean paste in a large saucepan with 6 cups (48 fl oz/1.5 L) water. Cook over medium–high heat, stirring, until paste dissolves and mixture begins to boil. Reduce heat to medium and add tofu, mushrooms and seaweed and simmer for 3–4 minutes.

Pour into individual cups or small bowls and set scallion slices and snow pea sprouts on top. Serve immediately.

Serves 4

Variation

Miso soup is versatile. Instead of seaweed, you can use baby English spinach leaves or basil or cilantro (coriander) leaves. Or add trimmed snow peas (mange-tout), sugar snap peas or baby green beans with the mushrooms, simmering until tender. Or flavor with julienned fresh ginger or thin slices of garlic when adding mushrooms.

Mushroom and cilantro soup

3 tablespoons light olive oil

1 yellow (brown) onion, chopped

2 cloves garlic, minced

1-inch (2.5-cm) piece fresh ginger, peeled and
  finely chopped

5 cilantro (coriander) roots, finely chopped

1 green chili pepper, finely chopped

3 tablespoons lime juice

3 cups (24 fl oz/750 ml) vegetable stock

3 cups (24 fl oz/750 ml) coconut milk

2 teaspoons fish sauce

1 lb (500 g) mixed button, enoki, shiitake, cremini
  and oyster mushrooms, sliced if large

2 cups (2 oz/60 g) cilantro (coriander) leaves

Heat 1 tablespoon oil in a large saucepan over medium–high heat. Add onion, garlic, ginger, cilantro roots and chili pepper and cook, stirring, until onion is soft, about 5 minutes. Add lime juice, stock, coconut milk and fish sauce and bring to a steady simmer. Simmer for 15 minutes.

Meanwhile, heat remaining oil in a frying pan over medium heat. Add mushrooms and cook, stirring, until soft, about 5 minutes.

Reserve some mushroom slices for garnish. Add remaining mushrooms and mushroom juice to soup. Add cilantro leaves. Working in batches, process soup in a food processor until smooth, 1–2 minutes. Return soup to saucepan and reheat over medium–high heat, about 2 minutes.

Serve immediately, garnished with reserved mushrooms.

Serves 4

MUSHROOM AND CILANTRO SOUP

Thai pumpkin and coconut milk soup

12 oz (375 g) pumpkin, peeled and cut into 1-inch (2.5-cm) pieces

2 tablespoons lime juice

1 large yellow (brown) onion, peeled and chopped

2 cloves garlic, chopped

2-inch (5-cm) piece fresh ginger, peeled and chopped

3 red chili peppers

1 stalk lemongrass, bottom 3 inches (7.5 cm) only, finely chopped

1 teaspoon dried shrimp paste

3 cups (24 fl oz/ 750 ml) coconut milk

1 cup (8 fl oz/250 ml) chicken or vegetable stock (see page 14 for step-by-step chicken stock)

1 tablespoon fish sauce

1/2 cup (1/2 oz/15 g) baby basil leaves, for garnish

Place pumpkin pieces in a large bowl and add lime juice. Stir to combine and set aside.

Place onion, garlic, ginger, chili peppers, lemongrass and shrimp paste in a food processor and process until smooth, 2–3 minutes. In a large saucepan, combine onion mixture with ¼ cup (2 fl oz/60 ml) coconut milk. Cook over medium–high heat until mixture is fragrant and reduced, about 5 minutes. Add remaining coconut milk, stock, and fish sauce and cook over medium–high heat, stirring, until liquid begins to bubble. Simmer for 5 minutes. Add pumpkin pieces and lime juice and simmer until pumpkin is tender, 10–15 minutes.

Ladle soup into individual bowls and serve sprinkled with basil leaves.

Serves 4

THAI PUMPKIN AND COCONUT MILK SOUP

Shredded cabbage soup

1 tablespoon peanut oil

1 teaspoon dried shrimp paste, optional

2 cloves garlic, peeled

1/4 teaspoon sea salt

8 black peppercorns

1 red chili pepper, seeded

1 cup (1 oz/30 g) cilantro (coriander) leaves

1 tablespoon lemon juice

2 teaspoons fish sauce

8 cups (64 fl oz/2 L) chicken or vegetable stock
(see page 14 for step-by-step chicken stock)

2 cups (6 oz/180 g) shredded Chinese cabbage

Combine oil, shrimp paste (if using), garlic, salt, peppercorns, chili pepper, cilantro, lemon juice and fish sauce in a food processor and process to a smooth paste, about 2 minutes.

Place paste in a large saucepan over medium heat and simmer, stirring, until fragrant, about 5 minutes.

Add stock and bring to a steady simmer. Simmer for 15 minutes. Add more lemon juice if the soup is not tangy enough or more fish sauce if it is not salty enough.

Add cabbage and simmer until cabbage is tender, 2–3 minutes.

Ladle soup into individual bowls and serve immediately.

Serves 4

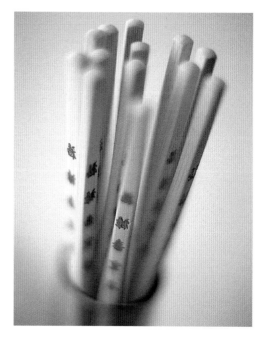

Mushroom wonton, noodle and spinach soup

9 oz (280 g) mixed oyster, shiitake and button
mushrooms

1/2 teaspoon white pepper

1/2 teaspoon sea salt

3 tablespoons chopped fresh cilantro (coriander)

1 tablespoon peeled and grated fresh ginger

2 cloves garlic, roughly chopped

1 fresh or 2 dried kaffir lime leaves, finely
chopped or 2 teaspoons finely grated lime zest
(rind)

4 water chestnuts, finely chopped

1 small egg, lightly beaten

20 wonton wrappers

8 cups (64 fl oz/2 L) chicken or vegetable stock
(see page 14 for step-by-step chicken stock)

1/2 lb (250 g) fresh egg noodles

8 oz (250 g) baby English spinach leaves or
shredded English spinach leaves

Combine mushrooms, pepper, salt, cilantro, ginger, garlic and kaffir lime leaf in a food processor and process until smooth, about 2 minutes. Transfer mixture to a bowl and stir in water chestnuts and egg.

Lay wonton wrappers on a dry surface and place 1 heaping teaspoon mushroom mixture in middle of each wrapper. Wet edges with a little water, using a pastry brush or your finger, and fold edges in to form bundles, pressing edges together to secure filling.

Place stock in a large saucepan over medium heat and bring to a steady simmer.

Bring a large pot of water to a boil. Add noodles and cook until tender, 5–7 minutes. Drain and rinse noodles and add to stock.

Add wontons to stock and simmer until cooked through, 5–6 minutes. Stir in spinach and cook until wilted, 2–3 minutes.

Ladle soup into individual bowls and serve immediately.

Serves 4

MUSHROOM WONTON, NOODLE AND SPINACH SOUP

Vegetable laksa

4 tablespoons light olive oil

2 small red chili peppers, finely chopped

3 cloves garlic, finely chopped

2-inch (5-cm) piece fresh ginger, peeled and grated

1 stalk lemongrass, bottom 3 inches (7.5 cm) only, finely chopped

1 teaspoon ground coriander

1/2 teaspoon turmeric

1 teaspoon dark brown sugar

1/4 cup (2 fl oz/60 ml) lime juice

3 cups (24 fl oz/750 ml) coconut milk

3 cups (24 fl oz/750 ml) vegetable or chicken stock (see page 14 for step-by-step chicken stock)

4 medium yellow tomatoes, cut into quarters

8 oz (250 g) fresh thick rice noodles

2 medium Asian eggplants (aubergines), cut diagonally into 1-inch (2.5-cm) pieces

1 small green bell pepper (capsicum), seeded and cut into thin strips

1 small yellow bell pepper (capsicum), seeded and cut into thin strips

5 oz (150 g) bean sprouts

1/4 cup (2 fl oz/60 g) crispy fried shallots (French shallots) (see page 58 for recipe)

Heat 2 tablespoons oil in a large saucepan over medium–high heat. Add chili peppers, garlic, ginger, lemongrass, coriander, turmeric and brown sugar and cook, stirring, until mixture is fragrant, 3–4 minutes. Add lime juice, coconut milk and stock. Increase heat to high and bring liquid to a steady simmer. Reduce heat to medium and simmer for 15 minutes. Add tomatoes and cook for 5 minutes.

Bring a large saucepan of water to a boil. Add noodles and cook until tender, about 3 minutes. Drain noodles and set aside.

Heat remaining oil in a heavy-bottomed frying pan over medium–high heat. Add eggplant slices in a single layer and cook until golden and cooked through, 3–4 minutes on each side.

Rinse noodles under very hot water, using a fork to separate them and place in individual bowls. Ladle soup over noodles and top with eggplant, bell peppers, bean sprouts and crispy fried shallots.

Serves 4

Vegetable pho

6 cups (48 fl oz/1.5 L) vegetable stock

6 cloves

4 black peppercorns

2-inch (5-cm) piece fresh ginger, peeled and
  sliced

1 cinnamon stick

2 star anise

4 cardamom pods

1 tablespoon fish sauce

8 oz (250 g) green beans, sliced

8 oz (250 g) thick asparagus spears, cut into
  2-inch (5-cm) pieces

8 oz (250 g) dried rice noodles

6 oz (180 g) chopped Chinese greens, such as bok
  choy or choy sum, or English spinach

4 sprigs mint

4 sprigs cilantro (coriander)

chili sauce, for serving

fish sauce, for serving

lime wedges, for serving

Combine stock, spices and fish sauce in a large saucepan over medium–high heat and bring to a steady simmer. Simmer until stock is infused with flavor, about 20 minutes. Strain through a fine sieve. Discard solids, return stock to saucepan over medium heat and simmer gently.

Bring a small saucepan of water to a boil. Add beans and asparagus and cook for 2 minutes. Drain, then set aside.

Place noodles in a bowl and cover with boiling water. Let stand until soft, about 5 minutes. Drain noodles and place in individual bowls. Top noodles with Chinese greens, cooked beans and asparagus, and mint and cilantro sprigs. Ladle stock into bowls.

Serve immediately, accompanied by chili sauce, fish sauce and lime wedges for each diner to add according to taste.

Serves 4

VEGETABLE PHO

Glossary

bok choy. Asian variety of cabbage with thick white stalks and mild-flavored dark green leaves. Sizes of bunches vary, from longer than celery stalks to baby bok choy about 6 inches (15 cm) long. Also known as Chinese cabbage. If unavailable, use Chinese broccoli or choy sum.

Chinese roast duck. Sold freshly roasted in Chinese markets and delicious in stir-fries or on its own. Use 1–2 days after purchase. Substitute roast chicken if unavailable.

choy sum. Popular and widely available Chinese green with yellow flowers and thin stalks. Every part of the mild-flavored vegetable can be used. Also known as flowering cabbage.

cilantro. Pungent, fragrant leaves from the coriander plant, resembling parsley and also called Chinese parsley and fresh coriander.

fish sauce. Pungent sauce of salted fermented fish and other seasonings. Products vary in intensity depending on the country of origin. Fish sauce from Thailand, called nam pla, is a commonly available variety.

kaffir lime leaves. Leaves from the kaffir lime tree generally used dried but also fresh to add an enticing citrus flavor and aroma to soups, curries and other simmered dishes.

lemongrass. Tropical grass whose pale stalks lend an intense lemon flavor to Southeast Asian dishes. Wrapped in a damp kitchen towel, lemongrass can be refrigerated for up to 1 month. The stalks, trimmed of the green blades, are bruised or chopped before use. Substitute grated lemon zest if lemongrass is unavailable.

miso. Thick paste of fermented ground soybeans, used in Japanese soups and other dishes. Light-colored varieties of miso are milder in flavor than dark-colored pastes.

oyster mushrooms. Creamy white mushrooms with fan-shaped caps, named for their resemblance to an oyster. Possessing a mild flavor, oyster mushrooms grow in the wild and are cultivated. Substitute button mushrooms if unavailable.

sambal oelek. Spicy Indonesian paste consisting of ground chili peppers combined with salt and occasionally vinegar. It can be used as a substitute for fresh chili peppers.

shiitake mushrooms. Meaty mushrooms with light or dark brown caps. Dried shiitakes, also available, need to be rehydrated. Soak, off heat, in boiling water for 10–15 minutes and squeeze dry before slicing or chopping.

shrimp paste. Produced by drying, salting and pounding shrimp into a pungent-flavored paste that is then formed into blocks or cakes.

udon noodles. Soft, creamy white, Japanese wheat flour noodle, available fresh or dried and in a variety of widths.

wonton wrapper. Thin sheets of wheat-based or egg-based dough, square or circular in shape, used to enclose a variety of fillings. Available fresh or frozen. Also called wonton skins or dumpling wrappers.

Index

Guide to weights and measures

The conversions given in the recipes in this book are approximate. Whichever system you use, remember to follow it consistently, thereby ensuring that the proportions are consistent throughout a recipe.

WEIGHTS

Imperial	Metric
⅓ oz	10 g
½ oz	15 g
¾ oz	20 g
1 oz	30 g
2 oz	60 g
3 oz	90 g
4 oz (¼ lb)	125 g
5 oz (⅓ lb)	150 g
6 oz	180 g
7 oz	220 g
8 oz (½ lb)	250 g
9 oz	280 g
10 oz	300 g
11 oz	330 g
12 oz (¾ lb)	375 g
16 oz (1 lb)	500 g
2 lb	1 kg
3 lb	1.5 kg
4 lb	2 kg

VOLUME

Imperial	Metric	Cup
1 fl oz	30 ml	
2 fl oz	60 ml	¼
3	90 ml	⅓
4	125 ml	½
5	150 ml	⅔
6	180 ml	¾
8	250 ml	1
10	300 ml	1¼
12	375 ml	1½
13	400 ml	1⅔
14	440 ml	1¾
16	500 ml	2
24	750 ml	3
32	1L	4

USEFUL CONVERSIONS

¼ teaspoon	1.25 ml
½ teaspoon	2.5 ml
1 teaspoon	5 ml
1 Australian tablespoon	20 ml (4 teaspoons)
1 UK/US tablespoon	15 ml (3 teaspoons)

Butter/Shortening

1 tablespoon	½ oz	15 g
1½ tablespoons	¾ oz	20 g
2 tablespoons	1 oz	30 g
3 tablespoons	1 ½ oz	45 g

OVEN TEMPERATURE GUIDE

The Celsius (°C) and Fahrenheit (°F) temperatures in this chart apply to most electric ovens. Decrease by 25°F or 10°C for a gas oven or refer to the manufacturer's temperature guide. For temperatures below 325°F (160°C), do not decrease the given temperature.

Oven description	°C	°F	Gas Mark
Cool	110	225	¼
	130	250	½
Very slow	140	275	1
	150	300	2
Slow	170	325	3
Moderate	180	350	4
	190	375	5
Moderately Hot	200	400	6
Fairly Hot	220	425	7
Hot	230	450	8
Very Hot	240	475	9
Extremely Hot	250	500	10

First published in the United States in 2000 by Periplus Editions (HK) Ltd.,
with editorial offices at 153 Milk Street, Boston, Massachusetts 02109 and
5 Little Road #08-01 Singapore 536983

Library of Congress Cataloging-in-Publication Data is available.
ISBN 962-593-936-9

DISTRIBUTED BY

USA
Tuttle Publishing
Distribution Center
Airport Industrial Park
364 Innovation Drive
North Clarendon, VT 05759-9436
Tel: (802) 773-8930
Tel: (800) 526-2778

Canada
Raincoast Books
8680 Cambie Street
Vancouver, British Columbia
V6P 6M9
Tel: (604) 323 7100
Fax: (604) 323 2600

Japan
Tuttle Publishing
RK Building, 2nd Floor
2-13-10 Shimo-Meguro, Meguro-Ku
Tokyo 153 0064
Tel: (03) 5437-0171
Fax: (03) 5437-0755

Southeast Asia
Berkeley Books Pte. Ltd.
5 Little Road #08-01
Singapore 53698
Tel: (65) 280-3320
Fax: (65) 280-6290

Set in Frutiger on QuarkXPress
Printed in Singapore

First Edition
06 05 04 03 02 01 00 10 9 8 7 6 5 4 3 2 1